SACRED MUSE

Books by Charles Scribner III

The Triumph of the Eucharist: Tapestries Designed by Rubens
Rubens
Bernini
*The Shadow of God: A Journey Through Memory, Art, and
   Faith*
Home by Another Route: A Journal of Art, Music, and Faith
Sacred Muse: A Preface to Christian Art & Music

Translations
Kirsten Liese, *Elisabeth Schwarzkopf*
Kirsten Liese, *Wagnerian Heroines [Wagnerheldinnen]*

Complete Bibliography: www.CharlesScribner.com

SACRED MUSE
A Preface to Christian Art & Music

CHARLES SCRIBNER III

ROWMAN & LITTLEFIELD
Lanham • Boulder • New York • London

Published by Rowman & Littlefield
An imprint of The Rowman & Littlefield Publishing Group, Inc.
4501 Forbes Boulevard, Suite 200, Lanham, Maryland 20706
www.rowman.com

86-90 Paul Street, London EC2A 4NE

British Library Cataloguing in Publication Information Available

Library of Congress Cataloging-in-Publication Data

Names: Scribner, Charles, 1951– author.
Title: Sacred muse : a preface to Christian art & music / Charles Scribner III.
Description: Lanham : Rowman & Littlefield, [2023] | Includes bibliographical references. | Summary: "This concise guide provides an introduction to the rich and variegated subject of Christian currents through art and music down the ages"— Provided by publisher.
Identifiers: LCCN 2022051048 (print) | LCCN 2022051049 (ebook) | ISBN 9781538178614 (paperback) | ISBN 9781538178621 (epub)
Subjects: LCSH: Christian art and symbolism. | Church music. | Arts, European—Themes, motives.
Classification: LCC NX650.C6 S39 2023 (print) | LCC NX650.C6 (ebook) | DDC 700/.4823—dc23/eng/20221125
LC record available at https://lccn.loc.gov/2022051048
LC ebook record available at https://lccn.loc.gov/2022051049

∞™ The paper used in this publication meets the minimum requirements of American National Standard for Information Sciences—Permanence of Paper for Printed Library Materials, ANSI/NISO Z39.48-1992.

In memory of three teachers and mentors:

Irving Lavin
John Rupert Martin
Julius S. Held

Contents

Sacred Muse

A Preface to Christian Art & Music

This short book is meant to provide an introduction to the rich and variegated subject of Christian currents through art and music down the ages; it is personal in its focus on favorite major artists and their subjects as examples of these sacred themes. My own professional focus on the Baroque giants Rubens and Bernini, who followed the revolutionary Caravaggio, explains— if not justifies—the central place they claim in this study. Indeed, my original plan was to write about that Baroque trinity in sacred art, but instead I have decided to place them in the context of the broader tradition. My focus is admittedly European—some might say Eurocentric—not global. My aim is to offer here a brief, illustrated book that may be read in one sitting. It is intended to be protreptic, something that will encourage and spur the reader—teacher, student, amateur—to pursue her or his own explorations in periods and artists that likewise hold special appeal.

THE NOTION THAT CREATION MIRRORS ITS CRE-
ator has special resonance for Christians; it has long been at the heart of our tradition, both explicitly and implicitly. It has even provided a basis of proof for the existence of God, the cosmological

argument proposed by the great Thomas Aquinas a millennium ago. The idea of a spontaneous creation ex nihilo without any agent—that is to say, without a Creator—is difficult for most mortals to imagine, however plausible it may be in principle to contemporary cosmologists. It runs counter to our experience. Our first appreciation of God, as we gaze up to the heavens, is as an Artist. Whatever else the universe may hold, its created shape and reflected glory suggest a vast canvas comprising a multitude of masterpieces.

The theme of creation has given rise to some of the greatest achievements by human creators in the realm of art. Arguably the most famous sacred work of art in Christendom is Michelangelo's great Sistine Chapel Ceiling, known to students and tourists alike long before they see it in the flesh. In his television series *Civilisation*, Kenneth Clark claimed "it is possible to interpret the whole of the Sistine Ceiling as a poem on the subject of creation." Thanks to its thorough cleaning and restoration three decades ago, it may now be experienced afresh, as it was when first unveiled to the impatient Pope Julius II. After the Vatican restorers removed five centuries of grime, candle smoke, and clumsy touch-ups, we may now view that ceiling

Michelangelo, *Sistine Ceiling*, Vatican (https://commons.wikimedia
.org/wiki/File:Vatican-ChapelleSixtine-Plafond.jpg)

once again ablaze with color—no longer "through
a glass darkly," in the vivid words of St. Paul, but
"face to face."

If one individual, and only one, could be chosen
to epitomize our notion of artistic genius, it would
be Michelangelo. Not only does he personify the
ideal of the Renaissance Man—three dimensional,
well rounded, like a sculpture—but he also towers
over the history of art just as his youthful *David*, the
marble embodiment of heroic virtue and virility, has
loomed over Florence for half a millennium.

Michelangelo, *David*, Accademia, Florence (https://www.wikiart.org/en/mich elangelo/david-1504)

Michelangelo was a prodigy. Yet, unlike the prodigies Bernini and Mozart, the source of his technical prowess has remained shrouded. Both Bernini and Mozart had professional artist/composer fathers to instruct them from the time they could walk. Michelangelo's father—too patrician to labor and too poor to provide any meaningful support—failed even to offer encouragement to the aspiring artist. "I sucked in chisels and hammers with my nurse's milk" is the only explanation Michelangelo was to offer in later years. As an infant, he had been farmed out to a stone cutter's wife, who served as his wet nurse. A teacher, Henry Adams once wrote, can never know the full extent of his influence: "a teacher affects eternity." That anonymous instructor who taught Michelangelo to wield a chisel indeed made a vital contribution to Western art.

Michelangelo was destined to live an extraordinarily long and productive life—eighty-nine years, almost two generations beyond the normal expectancy for that time. Yet what if our Florentine prodigy had survived no more than Mozart's thirty-five? He would still have left behind enough masterpieces to guarantee his preeminence in the annals of art. Among these we would find the Vatican *Pietà*, the

Bacchus, the *David*, and most of the Sistine Ceiling. The last would surely then be viewed as his *Requiem*, the masterpiece that, reluctantly undertaken, hastened the demise of its creator, who had protested in vain that he was a "sculptor, not a painter."

Vita brevis, ars longa. In Michelangelo's case, both life and art were long—and of enduring significance. It is nigh impossible to overestimate the influence of Michelangelo on later artists. While writing my books on Rubens and Bernini, the Castor and Pollux of the Baroque age, I found myself constantly invoking the name of Michelangelo— as did those artists themselves in both word and work. (A biographer of Rodin would say no less.) Arriving in Rome for the first time in 1601, the twenty-four-year-old Peter Paul Rubens proceeded to sketch figures from the Sistine Ceiling, rendering Michelangelo's heroic forms as sensuously and vividly as though they had been drawn from studio models, not copied from century-old frescoes some sixty feet overhead. A few years later, the painter Annibale Carracci advised the ten-year-old Bernini to study Michelangelo's *Last Judgment* for a full two years in order to get a firm grasp of anatomy.

"He was a good man, but he did not know how to paint." El Greco's appraisal represents the minority.

The founding fathers of the Baroque—Carracci, Caravaggio, and Rubens—owed Michelangelo an incalculable debt, and they paid him homage with their brushes. Poussin, Velázquez, and even Rembrandt may be cited among the beneficiaries of "the Homer of painting," as he was dubbed by Sir Joshua Reynolds, president of the Royal Academy. In his last discourse in London to his fellow academicians in 1790, Reynolds concluded, "I should desire that the last word which I should pronounce in this Academy, and from this place, might be the name of Michelangelo." A few years earlier, the German poet Goethe confessed in his *Italian Journey* that he had become so enthusiastic about Michelangelo that he lost all his taste for Nature, since he could not see her with the same eye of genius. Sir Thomas Lawrence, the British portraitist, supplied in 1819 a more biblical explanation: "God gave the command to increase and multiply before the Fall, and Michelangelo's is the race that might have been."

Steeped as he was in Neo-Platonic philosophy, which to the Renaissance mind was wholly compatible with Christianity, Michelangelo pictured mankind and divinity alike in idealized human form. "His people are a superior order of beings," concluded Reynolds. The prototype is Original

Michelangelo, *Creation of Adam*, Sistine Chapel, Vatican (https://en.wikipedia.org/wiki/The_Creation_of_Adam)

Man, naked Adam, that sensual revision of a classical river god who reaches out, languidly, to receive from his Creator the spark of a divine soul. Yet the artist's mind that gave immortal form to that perfect male remained conflicted and tormented, a soul yearning to escape the shackles of human flesh.

L'amor mi prende a la beltà mi lege ["love seizes me and beauty binds me"]—so Michelangelo described in verse, as in stone, his soul's struggle against its earthly chains. We are reminded of his unfinished marbles, those human forms that barely emerge from the confines of stone. Surely no artist in history has bequeathed so many unfinished masterpieces to the world. Far from being depreciated, those incomplete metamorphoses reveal, as no polished *Pietà* could reflect, the lifelong struggles that fueled his creativity. Such pain was the touchstone of Michelangelo's artistic growth. It was the process of creation, not the finely chiseled product, that progressively engaged his fertile imagination. In the Sistine Ceiling, he gave the very subject of Creation—beginning and end—its definitive epic form for our eyes to behold. These he did complete.

But Michelangelo was not alone in recomposing Creation. Almost three centuries later, he was answered in the thunderous chords, evocative harmonies, and soaring lines of an oratorio: *The Creation* by Franz Joseph Haydn. Composed by the prolific maestro well into his sixties, it represents Haydn's response to the Protestant Handel's *Messiah*, which so overwhelmed Haydn on his first hearing in 1791 at Westminster Abbey in London that he wept during the "Hallelujah Chorus." "He is the master of us all," was Haydn's verdict. Yet six years later he began to compose his own sacred masterpiece of comparable scope and power. A prequel of sorts to *Messiah*, Haydn's *Creation* sets to music an assemblage of texts derived, by an unknown librettist, from Milton's *Paradise Lost*. Then, in Vienna, the great patron of Baroque music Baron Gottfried van Swieten, who had earlier introduced Mozart to the music of Bach and Handel, provided a German translation for Haydn to set to the greatest music he would ever write. In his own words to his biographer, "I was never so religious as during the composition of *The Creation*. Daily I fell on my knees and asked God for strength."

The oratorio was hugely successful from the first hearing—so much for the mistaken notion that all great art must go unrecognized by contemporary society—and repeated countless times throughout Europe. Haydn's last public appearance was at a performance in 1808 in Vienna (his former pupil Beethoven was among the listeners) shortly before he died. At the climactic moment of Creation—the thunderous, exalting *fortissimo* of chords that accompany and overwhelm the words of God's command "And let there be light"—Haydn was himself so deeply moved that he confessed, "It was not I, but a Power above who created that."

Ever since I was a schoolboy soprano, my favorite chorus in all music was Haydn's triumphal setting of the opening of Psalm XIX, the climax of part one of his *Creation*: *Die Himmel erzählen die Ehre Gottes, und seiner Hände Werk zeigt an das Firmament* ["The heavens declare the glory of God, and the firmament proclaims his handiwork"]. Six decades later, this music still conveys, as no mere words can, the Creator behind Creation, just as Handel's soprano solo in *Messiah*—"I know that my redeemer liveth"—redeems the suffering of Job as well as our own and points forward, as an aural prefiguration, to Christ the Redeemer, our Messiah. As the Composer in Richard Strauss's opera *Ariadne auf Naxos* proclaims, *Musik ist eine heilige Kunst* ["Music is a holy art"]. But she is, fortunately, in good company throughout that worthy endeavor.

When my older son, Charlie, was two years old, I took him to kneel before the crèche set up for Christmas at our parish church. Gazing in wonder over the finely carved figures of the Holy Family, the shepherds, and the Magi gathered at the manger along with attendant animals, he finally sang out, "Ee-eye-ee-eye-oh!" My son may have mistaken the ownership of the farm, but he had no problem with animal iconography! Images speak with immediacy to the very young, as to us all.

I was reminded of another Charles, the narrator of Evelyn Waugh's novel *Brideshead Revisited*, whose magnificent translation to film I watched with my wife and newborn on PBS four decades ago (now available on DVD). In one early, idyllic summer scene on the terrace of "Brideshead," Charles challenges his eccentric and much-beloved new college friend Sebastian over the latter's troublesome convictions as a Catholic. Charles (played to the hilt by Jeremy Irons in the television series) dismisses it as "an awful lot of nonsense," but Sebastian retorts, "Is it nonsense? I wish it were. It sometimes sounds terribly sensible to me."

"But, my dear Sebastian, you can't seriously believe it all."

"Can't I?"

"I mean about Christmas and the star and the three kings and the ox and the ass."

"Oh, yes, I believe that. It's a lovely idea."

"But you can't believe things because they're a lovely idea."

"But I do. That's how I believe."

What brings us to the manger time and again? To the Mass? To faith? What about Sebastian's claim to believe something because it is a "lovely idea"? Is that nothing more than the intellectual equivalent to his beloved teddy bear, Aloysius (named after the young Jesuit saint)? Is truth more likely to be lovely? A theological argument might be fashioned in favor of this "lovely idea" based on the claim in St. John's gospel that God is both absolute Truth and absolute Love—an equation, as it were, that supports Sebastian's point. In retrospect, over the two millennia of Christianity, it appears that the Church implicitly adopted this notion insofar as it encouraged and commissioned artists to present its stories and theological claims in the most attractive and "lovely" fashions. By the time Christianity emerged free into the light of the Roman Empire, it decked itself and its core beliefs in the splendid raiment of visual art—architecture, painting, and sculpture.

St. Luke, evangelist and author of the book of Acts, was known to be a physician and hence became the patron saint of doctors and surgeons, as well as butchers and students—an arresting combination! But he was also the patron saint of artists, owing to an old tradition—unsupported by fact— that he painted the first icon, from life, of the Virgin Mary. Hence the many artists' guilds "of St. Luke" down the centuries. But that honor perhaps should have gone to the Apostle Paul, for it was Paul's wildly successful mission to the Gentiles throughout the Roman Empire that ultimately converted that empire and brought Christianity into the realm of its painters and sculptors—something that would have appeared alien to the first Jewish Christians, steeped as they were in the iconoclastic tradition of Judaism and its prohibition of "graven images" (a tradition that later took root in Islam and the stricter sects of Protestantism).

The first known Christian paintings date from two centuries after the death and Resurrection of Jesus—in the house church at Dura Europas in present-day Syria. There we find beautifully preserved frescoes (c. 235 AD) of Jesus as the Good Shepherd—the oldest surviving image of that most popular early Christian symbol—along with miracle scenes of Peter healing the paralytic and Jesus walking on water, and the Three Marys at the empty tomb of Jesus on Easter morning, among others. But the first full flowering of Christian art would have to wait another century and for a major military victory, that of the emperor Constantine at the Milvian Bridge in 312 AD.

Before battle, Constantine had a vision of a huge cross appearing in the sky along with a Greek inscription: "by this, conquer" (later rendered in Latin, *in hoc signo vinces* ["by this sign you shall conquer"]). He ordered his troops to display on their shields the Christian symbol of *chi-rho* (the first two Greek letters for "Christ"). The next year, the grateful, victorious emperor issued an imperial decree of tolerance, the Edict of Milan, for Chris-

tians throughout his empire as an end of persecu-
tion and the restoration of confiscated property. In
time his successors went further, declaring Christianity the empire's official religion. The Church had
finally become Roman—beyond all dreams.

During his transformative reign over both
Empire and Church, Constantine not only pre-
sided over the Council of Nicaea, which adopted
the Creed recited today, but also sponsored a huge
program of magnificent church building, from St.
Peter's in Rome to the Church of the Holy Sepulcher in Jerusalem. These huge basilicas—the term
comes from the Greek word for king, *basileus*—provided splendid gathering places for the Christian
faithful, now liberated to worship aboveground.
The catacombs along the Via Appia Antica had
small chapels decorated sparingly, if poignantly, by
frescoes of Christ and his saints, but the basilicas of
Constantine spared no expense in celebrating the
once-persecuted faith that was fast becoming the
official religion of Rome and her sprawling empire.
The new temples of the Christian God represented,
in effect, the pagan temples of classical antiquity—
think of the Parthenon—turned inside out.

Those pagan temples reflecting ancient worship
proclaimed their sacredness externally: the exteriors,

San Paolo fuori le Mura, Rome (https://commons.wikimedia.org/wiki/File:Rom,_Sankt_Paul_vor_den_Mauern_(San_Paolo_fuori_le_mura),_Innenansicht_1.jpg)

facing the public, were sheathed in marble columns and adorned with brightly painted relief sculpture. The Christian basilicas, by contrast, were designed to house congregations that assembled inside to worship their God in a participatory fashion. Hence the rows of magnificent marble columns were moved inside to reinforce the ceremonial procession from entrance to altar, while the wall surfaces were dematerialized by glowing mosaics and frescoes

Apse mosaic, San Vitale, Ravenna (https://commons.wikimedia.org
/wiki/File:Apse_mosaic_-_Basilica_of_San_Vitale_(Ravenna).jpg)

and punctuated by windows to illuminate this New
Jerusalem, a symbolic heaven on earth.

Imperial trappings of royal power were transferred to the worship of the new King of Kings. The
emperor's throne room became the hall of the New
Emperor, Christ. Whereas a Roman emperor sat
under a baldachin at the rear of his hall filled with
adoring subjects, Christ appeared, liturgically, in
the Sacrament under the baldachin or marble cibo-
rium at the altar at the climax of each Mass. Altar
replaced throne for this new heavenly emperor, who
ruled from a cross. Lest there be any doubt, monumental images of Christ now appeared in apses,
from Santa Pudenziana in Rome to San Vitale in

Ravenna, wherein Christ was bedecked with full imperial regalia: Christ as Emperor, *Pantocrator*, Ruler of the World.

At the same time, the pope, Christ's vicar on earth, likewise assumed imperial trappings as *Pontifex Maximus*, and over time the popes assembled a ceremonial court that would rival—and ultimately outlast—the secular emperor's, thus sowing the seeds of perennial conflict between Church and state down the ages to its climax in Napoleon's attack on the papacy. But that lay many centuries in the future.

The crowning glory of early Christian celebrations of Christ as Emperor are still preserved today in the mosaics of Ravenna, the seaport town on the Adriatic that for one brief shining moment served as capital of the Roman Empire in the West. Unrivaled in splendor and glittering detail, its fifth- and sixth-century mosaics—from Sant'Apollinare Nuovo to the Baptistery, to San Vitale and the mausoleum of Galla Placidia—belie any erroneous notion of artistic decline in the period of the so-called Dark Ages.

Even in the West, where the *Pax Romana* of a bygone empire had long given way to tribal warfare, and warlords had little use for architects and artisans, civilization—that is to say, the classical heritage of Greece and Rome—was preserved for later revivals by those diligent monks in Iona in western Scotland and in Ireland who kept vast libraries of ancient manuscripts and piously copied them while adding their own illuminations of fantastic decorative shapes and colors. (For a lively and unabashed treatment of this thesis, see Thomas Cahill's book *How the Irish Saved Civilization*. A more modulated, yet persuasive, view is offered by Kenneth Clark in *Civilisation*.) The epitome of these manuscripts is *The Book of Kells*, preserved at Trinity College in Dublin and visited by countless tourists. Its mazelike geometric patterns foreshadow the art of Frank Stella, the American abstract painter and sculptor who was influenced as a university student at Princeton by these early medieval illuminations.

On Christmas Day in the year of our Lord 800, the pope crowned Charlemagne—or Karl der Grosse or Carolus Magnus, depending on one's preferred tongue—emperor (*Imperator Augustus*) of a revived Roman empire in the West to rival the eastern emperor enthroned in Constantinople, the former Byzantium. Charlemagne is rightly considered the father of both the German and the French monarchies, but he was also, in a larger sense, the

The Book of Kells, Trinity College, Dublin (https://commons.wikimedia.org/
wiki/File:KellsFol034rChiRhoMonogram.jpg)

father of a united Europe. His palace in Aachen stands as a magnificent medieval successor to the sixth-century emperor Justinian's San Vitale in Ravenna, which Charlemagne saw and admired on his way back from Rome. His reign marked the first artistic renewal in the West, a consciously classical revival we know as the Carolingian Renaissance.

Charlemagne presented several relics to the Abbey of St. Sernin in Toulouse, which immediately established it as a worthy site for pilgrims to visit en route to Santiago de Compostela in Spain, which housed the head of the apostle James and lay at the hub of pilgrimage routes in Europe. Three centuries later, the abbey church of St. Sernin was completed in 1120, only forty years after it was begun in 1080.

Saint Sernin, Toulouse (https://commons.wikimedia.org/wiki/File :Nave_of_Basilica_Saint-Sernin_-_2012-08-24.jpg)

It rises as a magnificent monument to the style known as Romanesque, its towering nave crowned with a barrel vault—think of an inverted half-pipe from the Olympic snowboarding competition—supported by massive columns directing the thrust of tons of stone downward to earth. It is called a basilica, but it bears little resemblance to those of Rome. Rather, it epitomizes the "pilgrimage plan," a practical arrangement of side chapels radiating off a semicircular aisle behind the high altar and apse, to accommodate queues of passing pilgrims gaining valuable indulgences through their veneration of relics—a spiritual World's Fair pavilion. Two years into construction, the architect—or his best pupil—began work on the new Spanish pilgrimage church of Santiago de Compostela at the end of the line.

But high noon in the Middle Ages was yet to come, along with the full flowering of the Gothic style epitomized in France by the cathedral of Chartres, begun in 1194. The technical innovation of rib vaults and flying buttresses—to direct the downward forces outward, beyond the exterior walls, as well as downward—allowed builders to scale new heights and to dematerialize the walls with luminous stained-glass windows.

Kenneth Clark called Gothic cathedrals "hymns to the divine light." High Gothic was, in every sense

Chartres Cathedral (https://commons.wikimedia.org/wiki/File:Chartres
_-_Cath%C3%A9drale_16.JPG)

of the word, all about light, the Shadow of God. It achieved and reflected in all media, fully coordinated, a parallel spiritual universe, a retreat from the mundane world, a vision of Heaven on Earth.

Nowhere is this achievement of "sermons in stone" or "frozen music"—as Gothic cathedrals have evocatively been dubbed—better described and explained than in Émile Mâle's *The Gothic Image*. But others have also captured the magic. In *The Power of Myth*, Joseph Campbell muses about Chartres, "I'm back in the Middle Ages. I'm back in the world I was brought up in as a child, the Roman Catholic spiritual-image world, and it is magnificent. . . . That cathedral talks to me about the spiritual information of the world. It's a place for meditation, just walking around, just sitting, just looking at those beautiful things." As Albert Finney, playing an architect, says to Audrey Hepburn, his wife in the 1967 film *Two for the Road*, "Nobody knows the names of the men who made it. To make something as exquisite as this without wanting to smash your stupid name all over it. . . . All you hear about nowadays is people making names, not things." *Plus ça change*.

By the fourteenth century, the twilight of the Middle Ages offered the glimmer of a new dawn—

the Renaissance. Heralded in Italy by the painter Giotto, it rose to new heights of humanism in the late fifteenth and early sixteenth centuries in the art of Leonardo, Michelangelo, and Raphael. "Man is the measure of all things"—that famous proclamation of the ancient Greek philosopher Protagoras— became a new credo for artists and architects alike. The ideal of the human body was revived from classical antiquity and applied to architectural theory as well: buildings should evoke bodies. The new basilica of St. Peter's in the Vatican, designed to replace the now-crumbling Constantinian original, was to be crowned by a dome symbolizing the head, or crown, of Christendom.

The Renaissance life of the mind brought forth countless treatises on humanistic theory that spelled out a Christian humanism wholly compatible with faith. There was no "Da Vinci code"—in fact, no "Da Vinci" (he was always "Leonardo"). Any contemporary passerby would have recognized—from countless early Renaissance precedents—the young, beautiful disciple with long tresses beside Christ in the Last Supper as the future Evangelist John, the "beloved disciple." But they would surely not have posited, like perennial schoolboys, so many erections beneath the folds of drapery in images of the Dead

Dome, St. Peter's, Vatican (https://commons.wikimedia.org/wiki/File:Basilique_Saint-Pierre_Vatican_dome.jpg)

or Resurrected Christ. Brilliant scholar though he was, Leo Steinberg illustrated (in his *Sexuality of Christ in Renaissance Art and in Modern Oblivion*) the pitfalls of post-Freudian interpretations that conjure up overly erotic readings of such drapery folds and Christ's "slung leg" over his Virgin mother's lap (another salacious Steinberg inference) in Michelangelo's *Pietà*.

Michelangelo, *Pietà*, St. Peter's, Vatican (https://commons.wikime dia.org/wiki/File:Michelangelo%27s_Pieta_5450_cut_out_black.jpg)

It is not necessary to be a Catholic to understand faithfully the masterpieces of its art, but it is necessary to *think* like one and to shun anachronisms that obscure our understanding of the masters. The model here is D. W. Robertson's classic *A Preface to Chaucer*, wherein the great scholar applied the lessons of medieval iconography to reinterpret the satire and sense of the *Canterbury Tales* in the light and context of their time, not ours. Fidelity to the author or artist is as essential to today's scholars and teachers as fidelity to the composer is to conductors and singers. However challenging and contrary to our contemporary notions of spontaneity and creative deconstruction, it is required.

Marilyn Aronberg Lavin's magisterial elucidation of the complexity—from geometric to iconographic—of the Renaissance master Piero della Francesca sets the standard of this holistic approach to art in the tradition of the great Erwin Panofsky, especially in his studies of the early Lutheran giant of German art, Albrecht Dürer. More recently, she has clarified the most enigmatic and justly beloved Venetian masterpiece to have crossed the Atlantic: Giovanni Bellini's *Ecstasy of St. Francis* at the Frick Collection in New York. Long debated as a scene— in the most glowing of landscapes—of St. Francis

Bellini, *Ecstasy of St. Francis*, Frick Collection, New York (https://en.wikipedia.org/wiki/File:Giovanni_Bellini_-_Saint_Francis_in_the_Desert_-_Google_Art_Project.jpg)

receiving the stigmata, Lavin sets the matter to rest and demonstrates that it is not so; rather, it displays with stunning originality nature's miraculous response to Francis's total identification with Christ. Bellini's implicit dialogue between saint and nature, replete with Christian symbols, offers nothing less than his painterly response to Francis's famous canticle, the *Laudes Creaturarum*, his hymn to Creation.

Within a few years of the 1512 unveiling of the Sistine Ceiling, the high noon of the Renaissance was eclipsed by storm clouds: in 1517, Martin Luther nailed his ninety-five theses to the door of the Castle Church in Wittenberg. Though no one, least of all Luther, would have foreseen it at the time, this act was to set in motion a full-scale revolution that engulfed the Church and eventually most of Europe—the Protestant Reformation. A decade later, in 1527, Rome was brutally sacked by imperial troops and German Protestant mercenaries. The religious crisis sparked a parallel crisis of faith among artists, who soon retreated into fantasy and a style we call Mannerism—that most self-conscious and progressively *stylish* of styles that divorced art from nature in the works of Pontormo, Bronzino, Parmigianino, and their Netherlandish followers Goltzius, Spranger, and Cornelis van Haarlem. But, as in the case of postwar Abstract Expressionism four hundred years later, it was only a matter of time before a counterreaction took root, a return to basics—in this case, a return to nature and naturalism that followed the Counter-Reformation.

The great Titian in Venice offers a glowing exception to the stylistic excesses of the Mannerists. His mastery of heroic forms and stunning effects

Titian, *Assunta*, Frari, Venice (https://commons.wikimedia
.org/wiki/File:Tizian_041.jpg)

as a supreme colorist at the zenith of the Venetian Renaissance tradition produced the most brilliant affirmation in art of the doctrine of the Virgin's bodily Assumption into heaven. Too bold a claim? Not for the visitor to the Frari (Franciscan) church in Venice, where Titian's high altarpiece has proclaimed in convincing naturalism and sensuous contours that gravity-defying miracle for the past five hundred years. Something of a false dawn, it anticipates by a century the arrival of the High Baroque, just as it renders the infallible, ex-cathedra proclamation of that doctrine by Pope Pius XII in 1950 an anticlimax. Titian had already offered confirmation to open eyes half a millennium earlier.

At the same time, the second half of the sixteenth century witnessed the full flowering of polyphony in sacred music, which had begun to challenge the tradition of monophonic Gregorian and plainchant beginning in the late Middle Ages and through the Renaissance with composers Guillaume de Machaut, Josquin des Prez, William Byrd, and Thomas Tallis, among others. The last two were "unreformed" English Catholics who nonetheless retained their dominant positions as composers of sacred music for the English Protestant Church (and for the monarchs who otherwise persecuted

Catholics) because of their sheer talent—as well as diplomatic modulations. But the polyphonic crown belongs to Giovanni Pierluigi da Palestrina of Rome. He was the most famous composer of sacred music in his time, as he brought polyphony to its late Renaissance culmination, developed the practice of counterpoint, and set the stage a century later for the Protestant Johann Sebastian Bach, who studied and hand copied Palestrina's masses and even composed his own adaptation of the Kyrie and Gloria from Palestrina's *Missa sine nomine* in 1747.

As an emphatic response to the wave of icono-clastic Protestants who stripped Catholic churches and cathedrals of their altarpieces, sculptures, and stained-glass windows, the Council of Trent called on the Church to enlist an army of artists to defend doctrine through the alluring propaganda of their creations. As in the Middle Ages, art was once again to be the handmaid of the Faith. The Age of the Baroque, the zenith of didactic spirituality in art, was about to dawn—and where more fitting than in Rome?

No single artist did more to revolutionize and reform religious art than Michelangelo Merisi da Caravaggio (1571–1610). He was literally a "second Michelangelo" and well aware of the weight of his

Christian name. He did not fall short. This powerful genius from northern Italy broke into Roman art at the dawn of the Baroque like a bolt of lightning, electrifying his age and sending a current down through the art of the entire seventeenth century. He lived only thirty-nine years, his career confined to two decades and a few dozen major commissions; he had no workshop, no students or studio of assistants; yet he left an indelible imprint on artists to come: Rubens, Rembrandt, and Velázquez—to name just three of the brightest lights.

Caravaggio was controversial. In a *Who's Who* of painters, his police record would take first place; his antisocial behavior ranged from throwing a plate of artichokes at a waiter to killing a man on a tennis court (for which he had to flee Rome and travel in exile from Naples to Malta to Sicily). He was equally controversial in his art; few painters have provoked such extremes of praise and condemnation from their contemporaries. No major religious painter had so many altarpieces rejected—only to be snatched up by some of the most discriminating connoisseurs of the day. He was praised and damned for the same thing: his bold and often brutal naturalism, his revolutionary aim to paint the people and objects of the natural world as he saw them; to do otherwise, he claimed, would be but "bagatelles, child's play." He was begrudgingly admired—considered a useful reformer who restored naturalism to art, bringing it back down to earth after decades of flights of Mannerist fantasy, yet scorned as a revolutionary who went too far.

The seventeenth-century biographer and art critic Gian Pietro Bellori labeled Caravaggio a mere *imitatore della natura*, an imitator of nature who often "degenerates into low and vulgar forms." Among the paintings Bellori singled out as "failing in decorum" is the brilliant masterpiece painted around 1602, *The Supper at Emmaus*, today in the

Caravaggio, *The Supper at Emmaus*, National Gallery, London (https://commons.wikimedia.org/wiki/File:1602-3_Caravaggio,Sup per_at_Emmaus_National_Gallery,_London.jpg)

National Gallery in London, a tour de force of technique and innovation by the artist approaching thirty years of age.

Bellori castigated "the rustic character of the two apostles, the Lord who is shown young and without a beard, the innkeeper's failure to remove his cap, and a basket of fruit out of season" (for a biblical scene that took place the day after Easter, in springtime). Yet, three centuries later, the American abstract painter Frank Stella—one of the few with a deep knowledge of art history—wrote in the *New York Times*, "Abstraction today wants to make sure it can have everything Caravaggio served up in *The Supper at Emmaus*, a painting filled with projective gesture, psychological presence, and pictorial import."

Caravaggio followed both St. Luke's account of the post-Resurrection appearance (24:13–35) and the Venetian artistic tradition of showing the startled disciples recognizing Jesus at the moment he blesses the bread at their evening meal in an Emmaus inn—a pictorial variation and condensation of Leonardo's famous *Last Supper* in Milan. The Resurrected Christ's far-reaching gesture of benediction is framed by the thunderstruck disciples, the right one flinging his arms outward in the form of a cross as though to exclaim, "But Lord, you were crucified!" The Renaissance theorist Leon Battista Alberti wrote that the movements of the body reflect those of the soul, and therefore thought and feeling should be conveyed through outward gestures by artists. Caravaggio reveals himself as a master of psychological and dramatic rhetoric: his gestures speak louder than words.

But what of Bellori's complaints? Let's cross-examine him. First: the youthful beardless Christ, so unlike the familiar face of Jesus. The great Bernard Berenson called him "against all tradition and precedents, a boy preacher startling the yokels out of their wits." Yet this face—of a Resurrected Christ who *does not look like himself*—reveals Caravaggio's brilliant solution to the mystery of why these disciples had failed to recognize him, an original solution that he based on scripture. Saint Luke never fully explains why the disciples had failed to recognize Jesus after he joined them along the walk to Emmaus; he mentions only that "their eyes were kept from recognizing him." But at the end of St. Mark's gospel there is a brief reference to the appearance (16:12) that is both explicit and explanatory: he states that Christ appeared to the disciples *in alia effigie*—as the Vulgate renders it, "in another likeness."

Evidently this single phrase suggested to Caravaggio a solution to the problem of recognition. It also offered a biblical sanction for showing Christ in a different guise, *in alia effigie*, as the Evangelist describes him. Yet, by following Mark's lead and adopting a new face for Christ, Caravaggio intended not only to rationalize that miracle of recognition but also to *sacramentalize* it. This appearance at supper was traditionally interpreted by theologians as a confirmation of not only Christ's physical resurrection but also his bodily presence in the Eucharist, a doctrine of paramount importance to the Catholic Church of the Counter-Reformation. The doctrinal controversy between Catholics and Protestants over the nature of Christ's identification with the sacrament had by this time led to an intensified Catholic emphasis on the centrality of the Eucharist and the belief in the Real Presence. The Church reaffirmed this tenet of faith by every available means, including artistic representations of Eucharistic subjects such as the Supper at Emmaus. In the Jesuit book of engravings, Geronimo Nadal's *Evangelicae Historiae Imagines* (1593), the Supper at Emmaus was illustrated as a prefiguration of the Mass wherein Christ, as Priest, distributes the broken bread to his two disciples. Caravaggio intended his painted version to be no

Caravaggio, *The Supper at Emmaus* (detail), National Gallery, London (https://en.wikipedia.org/wiki/Supper_at_Emmaus_(Caravaggio ,_London)

less sacramental; rather, he sought a more visually persuasive way of conveying the same idea.

For Caravaggio, the disciples' recognition of Christ is achieved solely through the Eucharist. To underscore this point, he deliberately removed all other clues to Christ's identity; we look in vain for the nail prints or the side wound (later revealed to the doubting Thomas). His hands are so arranged that it is impossible to determine whether the wounds are there, and the garments cover his side. Most striking of all, Christ's face is not that of the Crucified, even at the moment of recognition. That recognition, therefore, is the result of his gesture alone, the extended hand blessing the bread, an allusion to the priest's act of blessing at the consecration of bread into the Body of Christ during the Mass. (Beside the loaf of bread are the vessels of water and wine, as on an altar.) Christ's sacramental gesture becomes the sine qua non of his self-revelation to his disciples, as if to stress that only through the Eucharist does Christ reveal himself both physically and spiritually to the faithful, now as then.

The particular likeness Caravaggio chose for this *alia effigies* harks back to the earliest type in Christian art, young and beardless, as found on the Junius Bassus sarcophagus, unearthed in Rome in 1595. The early Christian status of this Apollonian type (as distinct from the later, mature and bearded, Zeus type that took hold in art) provided historical justification for its adoption here at a time when the Counter-Reformation Church was

Sarcophagus of Junius Bassus (detail), Vatican Museums, Rome (https://commons.wikimedia.org/wiki/File:Tesoro_di_san_pietro ,_sarcofago_di_giunio_basso.JPG#mw-jump-to-license)

engaged in a revival of early Christian sources to buttress its historical and sacramental claims and to counter Protestant assertions that *they* were the true heirs to the early Christians. This type was revived during the Middle Ages and Renaissance; two important examples may have served as actual sources for Caravaggio.

One was a devotional painting (Galleria Borghese, Rome) based on a lost Leonardo of the *Salvator Mundi*, now attributed to Marco d'Oggiono but then thought to be a work by Leonardo himself; it hung in the bedroom of Pope Paul V as his most cherished painting. Like his counterpart at Emmaus,

Marco d'Oggiono, *Salvator Mundi*, Borghese Gallery, Rome (https://com
mons.wikimedia.org/wiki/File:Marco_d%27Oggiono,_Salvator_Mundi,_c
.1500,_Galleria_Borghese,_Rome.jpg)

the young "Savior of the World" is shown in the act of blessing, a gesture of salvation with clear sacramental overtones. This iconic image of an eternally youthful Christ offered to Caravaggio an esteemed prototype for his Savior at Emmaus—one who likewise reveals himself in a gesture of blessing.

According to Christian doctrine, salvation is inseparable from the Resurrection and the Second Coming of Christ, so it is singularly appropriate that an even more famous source for Caravaggio's Christ was also the most prominent scene of Resurrection and Judgment in Rome—by his illustrious namesake Michelangelo in the Sistine Chapel fresco, where high above the altar Christ appears at the end of time as a youthful, beardless deity. The two images share not only the facial type but also two crucial, contrapuntal gestures. In Michelangelo's fresco, Christ's right arm is raised while the left and less active one reaches across his side as if to point to his side wound. Caravaggio lowers the dramatically extended right arm as he transforms a gesture of judgment into one of blessing. But the left arm, relatively unaltered, recalls what is no longer visible: the side wound. These allusions to Michelangelo's Christ of the Last Judgment suggest a deeper link between the two subjects: the idea that Christ's

Michelangelo, *Christ* (detail of *Last Judgment*), Vatican, Rome
(Charles Scribner)

appearance to his disciples at Emmaus anticipates,
proleptically, his final appearance to mankind. Both
artists depict epiphanies of the Risen Christ.

Caravaggio's three primary sources for his
Christ *in alia effigie*—the early Christian type, the
Leonardesque *Salvator Mundi*, and Michelangelo's
Judge—all share a common referent: the image of
the eternal, divine Savior; not the earthly, historical
Jesus, but rather the heavenly, glorified Christ of
the Second Coming. To answer another of Bellori's
complaints, the innkeeper failed to remove his cap
in the Lord's presence precisely because he remains

outside this miraculous revelation, illumined by metaphysical light, the light of enlightenment. Yet his head casts a symbolic shadow—a negative halo, as it were—above Christ's head, where we might expect a more traditional one, perhaps here signifying that even those ignorant of Christ may yet honor him unconsciously. Likewise, the basket of fruit, admittedly "out of season," is richly symbolic with Eucharistic grapes, the apple of Adam's fall, and a pomegranate (an emblem of resurrection). Perched precariously at the table's edge, it casts a shadow in the form of a fish, the ancient symbol for Christ (since the letters of the Greek word for fish, *ichthus*, referred to "Jesus Christ, Son of God, Savior"). These symbolic shadows reinforce the metaphysical nature of Caravaggio's chiaroscuro, the juxtaposition of light and shadow, recalling the Latin maxim *Lux Umbra Dei* ["Light is the Shadow of God"].

The disciples are deliberately rustic, common humanity realistically rendered but dignified in their humility. One wears a cockle shell, the symbol of a pilgrim, as though to say, "We are all, even the lowliest of us, pilgrims on the way to Emmaus." Caravaggio was repeatedly criticized for populating his religious pictures with such ordinary people (most scandalous was the claim that he used a body of a drowned prostitute in Rome for the model of the Virgin Mary in his altarpiece *The Death of the Virgin* in the Louvre). One wag once remarked to me that he was sure Caravaggio would feel right at home on the New York subways. Yet he infused sacred subjects with a power and conviction, a humanity that is confrontational but equally reasonable: the disciples were all simple folk, unlike the high priests and Pharisees, the Establishment in Roman-occupied Palestine.

In his first *Supper at Emmaus*, Caravaggio reinterpreted a favorite subject of Renaissance art as a vivid confirmation of the Resurrection and the efficacy of the Eucharist. Basing his deceptively "unorthodox" representation of Christ *in alia effigie* on a verse in St. Mark's gospel, he fused into one image the earliest visual expression of Christ's divinity, the *Salvator Mundi*, and Christ at the Second Coming, whose triumphant revelation is accompanied by an impassioned reminder of the Crucifixion—two expansive gestures that break into the viewer's space. Here, in one of his very rare miracle scenes, Caravaggio confronts us with nothing less than an affirmation of salvation.

Among the artists who experienced Caravaggio's groundbreaking work firsthand in Rome was a young Fleming named Peter Paul Rubens. Like so many others from the north, he had journeyed to Italy to complete his training as a painter. He arrived in Rome in 1601. The timing could not have been more propitious. The Eternal City was being transformed by the Counter-Reformation popes into the artistic capital of Europe, a propagandistic assertion of their spiritual primacy. Caravaggio was completing his wall paintings of St. Matthew's life for the Contarelli Chapel in San Luigi dei Francesi, an overpowering public debut of his dramatic chiaroscuro, which was to leave its mark on Rubens.

An early sheet of Rubens's sketches in Rome (Getty Museum, Los Angeles) for a scene of the *Last Supper* reveals quotations from Caravaggio's *Calling of St. Matthew* and from his *Supper at Emmaus*, as the young Rubens (six years Caravaggio's junior) was compiling his vast visual vocabulary. Whether Rubens actually met Caravaggio in the flesh must remain conjectural; what is certain is that he was deeply impressed by Caravaggio's art and translated it into his own idiom, a blend of Italian and Flemish sources.

Caravaggio, *The Calling of St. Matthew*, San Luigi dei Francesi, Rome (https://commons.wikimedia.org/wiki/File:The_Calling_of _Saint_Matthew-Caravaggo_(1599-1600).jpg)

On his return home, Rubens transformed his Netherlandish heritage with reflections of antiquity, Michelangelo, Tintoretto, and Caravaggio in the first of his two great Antwerp triptychs, the *Raising of the Cross*, commissioned in 1610. Rubens broke triptych boundaries, as his heroic Crucifixion extends beyond the central panel to embrace the

Rubens, *The Raising of the Cross*, Cathedral, Antwerp (https://com mons.wikimedia.org/wiki/File:Peter_Paul_Rubens_-_Raising_of_the _Cross_-_1610.jpg)

two flanking wings in this dramatic affirmation of redemptive suffering.

His second triptych, begun a year later for the Harquebusiers—or Musketeers—Guild's altar in the cathedral, was the *Descent from the Cross*. By contrast, and in tune with its twilight subject, it expresses a stately serenity, poignancy, and classicizing equilibrium. As in the *Raising*, the famous ancient sculpture of *Laocoön* provides the central quotation from antiquity, as Rubens here adapted the figure of the suffering Trojan priest (in reverse) to the Priest/Victim Jesus being lowered from the

Rubens, *The Descent from the Cross*, Cathedral, Antwerp (https://commons.wikimedia.org/wiki/File:Descent_from_the_Cross_(Rubens)_July_2015-1a.jpg)

cross by his disciples. (Nicodemus, on the ladder, is a quotation of Laocoön's older son.)

The wings illustrate the Visitation, on the left, and the Presentation in the Temple, on the right; the outside shutters illustrate the medieval legend of St. Christopher and the Hermit. The unified iconographic program celebrates the guild's patron saint, Christopher. (The holy giant is based on an antique sculpture, the *Farnese Hercules*.) In keeping with the meaning of his Greek name *Christophoros* ["Christ-bearer"], he is shown carrying the Christ Child across a river at night, illumined by a lantern held by a hermit.

St. Christopher and the Hermit (triptych shutters), Cathedral, Antwerp (Charles Scribner)

Each of the three biblical subjects on the inside panels likewise illustrates the bearing of Christ. In the Visitation, the Virgin carries Christ in her womb as she visits her cousin Elizabeth; in the Presentation, the high priest Simeon holds the Christ Child as Mary raises her arms to receive him, a gesture poignantly varied in the central panel, wherein as Mater Dolorosa [Mother of Sorrows] she reaches up to hold her dead Son. Together the three panels present a gradual rightward descent in counterpoint to the central lowering of the Dead Christ along a suspended sheet of incomparable whiteness. At first viewing, Sir Joshua Reynolds commented, "None but great colorists can venture to paint pure white linen near flesh." A century later, Eugène Fromentin summed it up: "Everything is restrained, concise, laconic, as if it were a page of Holy Scripture."

The central Eucharistic doctrine of the Counter-Reformation had affirmed both the re-Presentation of Christ's sacrifice in the Mass and the Real Presence of Christ in the sacrament received by the faithful at the altar. Nowhere were those beliefs conveyed with such conviction and pathos as in Rubens's triptych that opened over an altar in Antwerp's cathedral, where it still bears eloquent witness today.

After the Eucharist, the sacrament of Penance—the ritual confession and absolution of sins—was of foremost concern to the Counter-Reformation. The rejection of sacramental confession by Protestants led to an insistent promotion through every available means: sermons, treatises, and the visual arts.

Following the doctrine's emphatic reaffirmation at the Council of Trent, images of penitent saints proliferated in altarpieces, prints, and paintings for private devotion. In his brilliant *Christ and the Penitent Sinners* (Alte Pinakothek, Munich), the work that first converted me as a college student to this artist,

Rubens, *Christ and the Penitent Sinners*, Alte Pinakothek, Munich (Charles Scribner)

Rubens combined two of the most popular penitent saints, Mary Magdalene and St. Peter, with the less frequently illustrated Good Thief and King David in a *sacra conversazione* of extraordinary grace and lyricism. This glowing picture reveals the culmination of the artist's Antwerp decade (1609–1620) of religious paintings for public commissions and private patrons.

The composition is defined by the diagonal S-curve of the radiantly blond Mary Magdalene kneeling before the Risen Christ, recalling their previous juxtaposition in *Descent from the Cross*. In both paintings, he emphasizes Mary Magdalene's long, Titianesque tresses, with which she had dried the Savior's feet before the Passion. Christ is presented in classical perfection like some Greco-Roman god—a combination of Apollo and Jupiter. His brilliant red toga contrasts with Mary Magdalene's off-white garment. Arms crossed over her breasts, she is here identified with the woman taken in adultery whom Jesus saved and admonished to "go and sin no more." Behind Mary stand three biblical penitents, bridging both testaments and beckoned by Christ. Closest to the Savior, weeping and with hands clasped, St. Peter reenacts his repentance for thrice denying his Master. The background rock recalls Christ's promise to him: "You are Peter and upon this Rock I shall build my church," an image and text invoked by the Roman Church in defense of the primacy of its first bishop and his papal successors. Identifiable by his crown is David—king, psalmist, and penitent adulterer. At the far left, holding a cross parallel to Christ, is the Good Thief, to whom Jesus at the Crucifixion promised a place in Paradise. His pose is an evocative quotation of Michelangelo's *Risen Christ* in Santa Maria sopra Minerva in Rome.

Rubens's emphasis on the encounter between Christ and Mary Magdalene is derived from the iconography of the *Noli Me Tangere* ["Do not touch me"], the Risen Christ's first appearance to Mary Magdalene on Easter morning, as described by the Evangelist John. Close as they are, they do not physically touch. Rubens's stress on the *visual* experience reaffirmed the function of religious art as prescribed by the Council of Trent: to evoke a lively sense of faith in the beholder. Here Rubens's emphasis is not so much on the act of penance as on the receptive gesture of the Risen Christ, a confirmation of Job's faith: "I know that my Redeemer liveth." Rubens combines heroic forms and sensuous surfaces to confirm, most invitingly (even seductively), his own affirmation of salvation.

Nowhere does Rubens offer more inventive variations on a religious theme than in his several Adorations of the Magi—a series of Epiphanies that reach a High Baroque climax in the 1624 altarpiece for the Norbertine Abbey of St. Michael's in Antwerp. His first version, also his first major commission in 1609 on his return to Antwerp from Rome, was for the *Staatenkammer* [Chamber of States] in the town hall—a nocturnal procession with shades of Caravaggio, Elsheimer, and the Venetians that provided a stately backdrop for the signing of the Twelve Years' Truce between the two Netherlands, North and South. For the high altar of St. Michael's, where Rubens had earlier provided an altarpiece for his mother's tomb, he shifted the time to midday for his most joyous—and liturgical—interpretation of the biblical subject. Rubens is said to have painted it in a week, surely an exaggeration. Yet the lively brushwork reveals a new fluidity and breadth, as though he had adapted the style of a spontaneous oil sketch to a full-scale painting. However rapid the execution, the composition was carefully prepared by his *modello*, or oil sketch (Wallace Collection, London), wherein he introduced a powerful centripetal grouping around the visually arresting Moorish king. The host of worshippers descends in a reverse

Rubens, *Adoration of the Magi*, Royal Museum, Antwerp (Charles Scribner)

S-curve from camels, alluding, as Julius Held noted, to the liturgy for the Feast of the Epiphany: "Multitudes of camels shall cover thee, dromedaries of Midean and Epha" (Isaiah 60:6).

Rubens's iconography—his language of images—reflects the liturgical function of the altarpiece as backdrop to the celebration of the Mass. Unlike the artist's earlier versions and his preliminary *modello*, the foremost king no longer offers gold; he is now robed in splendid ecclesiastical vestments as though he were a priest kneeling before the sacrament on the altar. The Virgin is rotated to a frontal view as she displays the body of Christ, whose reclining pose prefigures the *Pietà*. The close association of nativity and death was common throughout early Netherlandish altarpieces, which likewise employed "disguised symbolism" in the straw (bread), the ox (sacrifice), and the wooden crate with white cloth (altar), together alluding to the Eucharistic sacrifice of the Mass.

Rubens's propagandistic imagery extended to the original marble frame and sculptures, dismantled two centuries later but still preserved in the parish church of St. Trudo (Groot Zundert, Netherlands). The pediment was originally crowned by three alabaster statues designed by Rubens, each symbolizing the triumph over evil and heresy. St. Michael defeats Satan; the Virgin crushes the Serpent underfoot; St. Norbert stands victorious over the prostrated heretic Tanchelm, who in the twelfth century had denied the sacrament, church hierarchy, the paying of tithes, and ritual. It is precisely these pre-Protestant denials by Tanchelm that Rubens reversed in his resolutely Roman epiphany. In the painting, ancient Rome is personified by two soldiers beside a Corinthian column entwined with ivy, symbolizing its supplanting and renewal by the Church; the universality of the new Roman (Catholic) Empire is embodied in the assembly of witnesses—including an African, an Indian, and an Asian—from the equestrian knight to the beggar below him. In this Flemish Baroque feast for the eyes, Rubens reorchestrates his Netherlandish heritage and Italian influences with operatic grandeur. Centuries later, we can almost hear Handel's joyous chorus from *Messiah*, "For unto us a Child is born," resounding through the paint.

But Rubens did not limit himself—or his studio—to paintings. He was equally famous as an impresario of vast decorative programs. For the Jesuit church in Antwerp, he designed architecture, sculpture, altarpieces, and some thirty-nine ceiling paintings to rival those of Titian, Tintoretto, and Veronese in Venice. The day after the church dedication in 1621, Rubens wrote to William Trumbull, an agent of both King James I of England and his son Charles, Prince of Wales: "I confess that I am, by natural instinct, better fitted to execute very large works than small curiosities. Everyone according to his gifts; my talent is such that no undertaking, however vast in size or diversified in subject, has ever surpassed my courage." Brave words—but true.

Commissioned in late 1625 by Rubens's patron the Infanta Isabella, governor of the Spanish Netherlands, the *Triumph of the Eucharist* represents not

Rubens, *Triumph of Ecclesia* tapestry, Descalzas Reales, Madrid (Charles Scribner)

only Rubens's largest tapestry cycle (some twenty magnificent hangings) but also his most sumptuous and complex program of church decoration. The tapestries remain today at their original destination, the convent of the Descalzas Reales in Madrid. The program, an epic history of the Sacrament, comprises eleven large tapestries illustrating Old Testament prefigurations, allegorical victories, a triumphal procession, and a retinue of saints—all culminating in an apotheosis at the high altar.

The eleven narrative scenes feature fictive tapestries hung within illusionistic architecture—in other words, tapestries within tapestries. Both this double illusion and the bilevel architectural framings were unprecedented in tapestry design: the upper tapestries, framed by Solomonic columns, were designed to be viewed from below; the lower, framed by banded Doric columns, at eye level. Here in my original reconstruction of the oil sketches, a Eucharistic victory is coupled with an allegorical triumph. Above, Father Time, holding his scythe, raises his daughter Truth over an ecclesiastical battlefield strewn with defeated heretics: Luther, Calvin, Arius, and Tanchelm, among others. Surrounded by smoke and fire-breathing monsters, she points to a banderole inscribed (in the final tapes-

Rubens, *Truth* and *Faith* oil sketches, Prado, Madrid (Charles Scribner)

try) with the words of consecration, *Hoc est Corpus meum* ["This is my Body"].

The image of Naked Truth uplifted by Time was common currency in seventeenth-century political and religious propaganda. Here religious Truth is shown more modestly clothed. The scene recalls the emperor Constantine's proclamation after the Council of Nicaea: "The splendor of Truth has dissipated at the command of God those dissensions, schisms, tumults, and so to speak deadly poisons of discord."

Directly below, the personification of the Catholic Faith raises her chalice and host, a dramatic gesture paralleling Truth's directly above. In the air, putti carry emblems of the Passion. Behind the angel-drawn carriage march Faith's captives in tow: Science (with an astrolabe), Philosophy (with the features of Socrates), Nature (with multiple breasts), Poetry (with laurel crown), and exotic heathen. These figures personify some chief concerns of the era: the proper relationships between Faith and Science, Faith and Nature, and Faith and Reason, here described hierarchically as a sacred victor leading a retinue of captives. Rubens's revival of ancient triumphs represents the Baroque culmination of a Renaissance tradition starting with Petrarch's poem

I trionfi [*The Triumphs*], which soon pervaded art, literature, liturgy, and civic celebrations.

Rubens's unique framing device of fictive tapestries hanging within simulated architecture reveals different levels of illusion and reality. The tapestry of Faith is hung by "real" putti who cast shadows against the woven sky. Assembled within the convent chapel, these eleven fictive tapestries recall the eleven curtains surrounding the Holy of Holies in the ancient Jewish Temple, an allusion reinforced architecturally by the Solomonic columns. Beyond their decoration as extravagant liturgical wall hangings, Rubens's Eucharist tapestries created nothing less than a unified vision of sacred architecture within which he staged his most triumphal affirmation of his faith.

Rubens is an artist's artist; his influence down the centuries is legendary: Van Dyck, Jordaens, Watteau, Boucher, Fragonard, Gainsborough, Delacroix, Renoir—each paid him homage with their brushes. Even such unlikely heirs as Cézanne and Matisse studied him and painted copies of his masterpieces. Yet the "painter's Rubens" represents but one side of this multifaceted genius. His contemporary and friend General Spinola said of him, "Of all his talents, painting is the least." Renowned throughout Europe as a diplomat, Rubens negotiated peace between England and Spain, for which service he was knighted by both kings. He was also a dedicated scholar and Christian humanist, a learned classicist and antiquarian, a prodigious correspondent (in several languages), an amateur architect—in short, a true Renaissance man. His nephew described his life as "but one long course of study." The court chaplain at Brussels eulogized him as "the most learned painter in the world."

Rubens was a devout Catholic, a loyal subject of the Spanish Hapsburgs, a devoted husband, the father of eight children, and a prosperous, energetic, life-loving, thoroughly balanced man who lived in harmony with his society and, we may assume, with himself. No one could be further from the modern conception of the struggling artist who pays dearly—economically, spiritually, and socially—for exerting his genius. The very qualities with which Rubens was blessed tend to detract from his popular appeal today. Modern society prefers to find genius in a tormented Michelangelo, a rebellious Caravaggio, a withdrawn and introspective Rembrandt. Hollywood has yet to project Rubens's exemplary life onto the big screen.

There is another issue. Because Rubens was, like so many religious artists down to the nineteenth century, a *literary* artist—that is to say, a visual artist who faithfully interprets and translates texts into images—the student who would strive to understand his achievements within this religious tradition must at least be biblically literate. One need not have a graduate degree in theology, but one must know both testaments as well as the fundamentals of the faith: the core beliefs, the saints, the liturgy, and basic church history and structure—the very things that fifty years ago every elementary school pupil knew before receiving confirmation. Times have changed, but the groundwork required for a true appreciation of timeless sacred art has not. One cannot read French poetry without knowing French; one cannot read a classic religious painting without having basic biblical and theological knowledge.

If Rubens is underrated by modern sensibilities, the same cannot be said for his northern—and Protestant—counterpart Rembrandt, for whom the Bible was the primary source of pictorial inspiration. He is rightly considered *the* biblical illustrator par excellence. No painter ever probed more the depths of artistic inquiry into those sacred texts, which have provided the main wellspring of narrative representation for the past millennium in Western art.

In Rembrandt's case, his art stands apart from that tradition insofar as it was not the result of official commissions. The Calvinist Reformed Church that dominated the Dutch provinces prohibited artistic representation of religious subjects; ecclesiastical commissions that engaged Rubens were unavailable to the Protestant Rembrandt. Thus his treatment of biblical subjects in paintings, etchings, and—above all—private drawings reveal a personal, introspective expression of the artist's spiritual insights as he confronted the Bible as a skilled (if intuitive) exegete. He isolated each subject's core of meaning, its *kerygma*, and translated it into visual terms.

Rembrandt was unusually selective in his choice of subjects, with several traditional themes notably absent; we find no Last Judgments, Transfigurations, Weddings at Cana, or Bestowing of Keys on St. Peter. No doubt this Protestant artist chose to avoid subjects that had become closely associated with Catholic doctrines and the propagandistic imagery of the Counter-Reformation. At the same time, we find recurrent themes that, with no overtly theological or Protestant thrust, clearly appealed to Rembrandt's imagination, his creative response to the Bible, and its probings of the human condition: episodes from the Book of Tobit, the parable of the

Prodigal Son—or, more accurately in Rembrandt's conception, the Forgiving Father—and, above all, the Supper at Emmaus. His many treatments of the third topic reveal over three decades an evolution of both style and reflections on this Gospel account of divine revelation.

Rembrandt's early versions of the Supper capture the high drama we found exploited to the fullest in Caravaggio's London painting. But Rembrandt's masterpiece in the Louvre, painted in 1648, reveals something new, a reformed vision that sums up his genius. All traces of surprise and dramatic action have subsided, now replaced by a more contemplative scene. Behind the table, Christ looks upward as he quietly breaks bread; he is not the triumphant figure of Resurrection, but rather the Man of Sorrows, still evoking the pathos of his Passion and the grave. Around his head glows a diffuse nimbus as a halo, a muted contrast to earlier examples of a flash of light and sudden recognition. For these two disciples, that recognition emerges from a gradual interior awareness of his identity—and divinity.

At the left, one disciple raises his hands in a gesture of prayer and adoration, his back turned to the viewer. At the right, the older disciple draws back, looking in wonder at Christ. As Kenneth

Rembrandt, *The Supper at Emmaus*, Louvre, Paris (https://commons
.wikimedia.org/wiki/File:Rembrandt_The_Supper_at_Emmaus.jpg)

Clark has noted, this disciple is derived from
Leonardo's *Last Supper*, which Rembrandt knew
via prints (as well as copies in oil) from which he
produced several sketches a decade earlier. Thus
Leonardo's figure of Judas recoiling from Christ's
announcement of betrayal is transformed into

the embodiment of the shock of recognition. In view of Rembrandt's fascination with the great Leonardo masterpiece, the obvious question arises: Why did he himself never paint a Last Supper? Clark speculated that Rembrandt avoided subjects (the Annunciation is another) "in which the formal possibilities were exhausted."

Yet there may be another, more telling reason for that avoidance: Rembrandt's natural reluctance to treat a religious subject that by this time had become so weighted with Catholic and Protestant disputes over its meaning—the debates over the true nature of the Eucharist. The shift in the iconography of Last Suppers in Catholic art before and after the Council of Trent—from a scene of the Announcement of Betrayal to the Institution of the Sacrament, or Communion of the Apostles—underscores the Church's deliberate exploitation of that popular subject to reinforce its doctrinal insistence on the Real Presence in the face of Protestant denials.

In this context, Rembrandt's preference for the Supper at Emmaus—literally the "last supper" in the Gospels—takes on a new light. The twilight Emmaus story evokes none of the theological controversy surrounding the Last Supper. Rather, it offers a simple and direct expression of Christian faith, one that appealed to Rembrandt's appreciation of Mennonite simplicity. In his seminal study *Rembrandt and the Gospel*, the Dutch Protestant theologian Willem Visser 't Hooft finds in Rembrandt's interpretation of the Emmaus miracle the artist's visual assertion of "the eternal presence of Christ and the community of believers with him." In contrast with earlier interpretations, the Louvre painting reveals the disciples as overcome less by the shock of recognition and more "by the fact that the Lord is really alive, really present, and that they may share in his life." The tradition of associating Emmaus with a communion meal dates back to St. Augustine. In contrast with the Catholic Last Suppers equating that meal with the Mass, Rembrandt's *Emmaus* presents the Protestant response: a simple communion *meal* at which Christ is present "whenever two or three are gathered together" in his name.

What, then, are we to make of the vast niche that opens up behind the figure of Christ? Compositionally it monumentalizes and accentuates the centrality of Christ, an effective backdrop of chiaroscuro for his glowing nimbus. Titian had used a similar device in his late *Pietà* in the Accademia in Venice to enshrine the body of the Dead Christ. In his variation on that theme, Rembrandt introduced this vast, hollow backdrop of stone as a reference to the tomb—that dark region of death and oblivion—from which Christ emerged alive to rejoin his disciples.

That same year, 1648, Rembrandt—or a most talented (if anonymous) pupil under his supervision, according to more recent reattributions—painted a

Rembrandt (or pupil), *The Supper at Emmaus*, Staten Museum, Copenhagen (https://commons.wikimedia.org/wiki/File:The_supper _at_Emmaus,_pupil_of_Rembrandt,_1648,_Statens_Museum_for _Kunst_(Copenhagen,_Denmark).jpg)

second version of the subject, today in Copenhagen's Staten Museum, wherein the architectural background was replaced by a blank wall. The most striking aspect of this more modest painting is the introduction of a painted illusionistic curtain hanging in front of the picture and pulled back—but not completely—at the left. Such curtains were common in contemporary Dutch houses as protective coverings for paintings. Two years earlier, Rembrandt had included such a cloth in his painting of the Holy Family (Gemäldegalerie, Kassel)—a motif that can be traced back to Raphael's *Sistine Madonna*—in order to create a sense of intimacy in Rembrandt's domestic scene, as if the viewer has just pulled back the curtain to catch a glimpse of the family in their everyday surroundings. In the Emmaus painting, that curtain provides a sense of intimacy wholly appropriate to the subject.

Yet the curtain is not completely open. Part of the "canvas" (the painting within the painting) remains concealed, as if the viewer has paused to contemplate the revelation therein. Perhaps that curtain refers to Revelation itself, as Rembrandt explored it in his later works: a gradual awareness, an internal enlightenment, as subtle and silent as drawing aside a cloth. Luther's metaphor for the

Real Presence was the removal of a veil or curtain from the Sacrament, after which Christ would become inwardly visible to the faithful who received it—in contrast to the Catholic doctrine of Transubstantiation, a dramatic transformation at the moment of consecration. Rembrandt probably did not know of Luther's metaphor; his own exegesis of scripture led him to a visual equivalent wholly suited to the recognition of Christ's Real Presence at Emmaus. Two geniuses of spiritual insight—and *reformulation*—thus met in the realm of the imagination, the life of the mind.

Rembrandt offers a telling contrast to Rubens, whose work he studied and, in his early years, emulated. Rembrandt's mature explorations of the Gospels are as private and introspective as Rubens's are public and extroverted. Together they represent the Baroque summit of sacred interpretations in paint. Yet Rubens, like Michelangelo, ventured beyond two dimensions as he exploited the potential of space to engage the senses and religious responses. As impresario of decorative programs and multimedia productions, Rubens was peerless in northern Europe; for his counterpart, we must look south, a generation later, to the great Italian maestro Gian Lorenzo Bernini.

Bernini personified the Baroque style and era. He dominated the seventeenth century. His audience comprised Europe's leading patrons, prelates, and princes, but Rome was his stage—and stage enough. Bernini's monumental presence throughout the Eternal City remains as resonant as the ancient ruins. In marble, travertine, bronze, stucco, and gilt—in paint, through glass and shimmering water, sculptured space, and channeled light—Bernini left his imprint on the Catholic capital, the indelible stamp of genius. Within its walls he created another realm, one of imagination incarnate, which centuries later still shapes our experience of Rome and transfigures it.

According to his earliest biographers, Bernini was "the first to attempt to unite architecture with painting and sculpture in such a manner that together they make a beautiful whole [*un bel composto*]." To this end, he would "bend the rules without actually breaking them." This unification of the arts was Bernini's own concept. Though he wrote no treatise, he left a brilliant illustration of his theoretical views and their fulfillment in a small chapel of Santa Maria della Vittoria in Rome.

In 1647, Cardinal Federico Cornaro commissioned a memorial chapel for his illustrious Venetian

Bernini, Cornaro Chapel, Santa Maria della Vittoria, Rome (https://en.wikipedia.org/wiki/Ecstasy_of_Saint_Teresa)

family, which had supplied six cardinals and a doge; five years later, it was completed—Bernini's most famous, and telling, masterpiece. Thanks to the great Bernini scholar Irving Lavin, it may finally be understood fully in all its multifaceted brilliance.

Cornaro's close ties with the Discalced Carmelites and his special devotion to their founder, St. Teresa of Avila, gave rise to the central subject: Teresa's vision of an angel piercing her heart with the flaming arrow of Divine Love, an event that had been cited at her canonization in 1622. The white marble altarpiece, executed by Bernini's own hand, is enshrined within polychrome decoration that transforms the shallow chapel into a multilevel depiction of heaven. Bernini grouped the eight Cornaro figures four on a side—spanning two centuries—and shows them discussing and meditating about an apparition set deliberately beyond their sight lines: "Blessed are they that have not seen, yet believe." These animated, marble "donor portraits" are set against illusionistic reliefs of colonnaded and vaulted transepts (or perhaps heavenly corridors—they are not theater boxes, as so often described) directly above the wooden doors of Death.

Two colorful roundels of inlaid marbles in the pavement below show skeletons arising from the crypt. In the vault, overhead, frescoed clouds and angels spill over the architectural fabric of the chapel and stucco illustrations of Teresa's life—a metaphysical intrusion into the viewer's space. The heavenly aura, painted by Bernini's collaborator Abbatini, is realized below by sunlight passing through tinted glass before materializing into a blaze of gilded bronze shafts. These illumine the cloud-borne saint and angel in a metamorphosis of reflected light, the "Shadow of God." The gilded

bronze altar relief of the *Last Supper* at the wor-
shipper's level marks the Eucharistic significance of
Bernini's re-created miracle: the transubstantiation
of earthly matter into divine substance completes
the meaning of Bernini's sacred *bel composto*. Sculpture and painting are complemented architecturally by the marble tabernacle in which St. Teresa's
transverberation (mystical piercing) is exposed to
the faithful like a gleaming Host suspended in a
giant monstrance. With its hidden source of fil-
tered light, this temple in miniature anticipates
Bernini's full-scale oval church of Sant' Andrea al
Quirinale, "the work which displeased him least,"
where Bernini himself used to pray each day to find
peace and solace. Through the interplay of concave
and convex shapes, the pediment of heaven's portal
bows outward as if in response to the spiritual force
within. The divine text, recorded by Teresa and here
spun into the timeless shape of illusion, is inscribed
on a banderole suspended by angels above the
arch over the chapel: *Nisi coelum creassem ob te sola
crearem* ["If I had not created heaven, I would create it for you alone"].

Within the columned aedicule of variegated
marbles, Bernini admits the viewer to an intimate
vision of this sixteenth-century Spanish mystic, the

moment at which the beautiful young angel has withdrawn his golden arrow from Teresa's breast. Filled with the love of God, Teresa swoons, unconscious, elevated on a cloud, her lips parted, her limp hand dangling at her side. As befits the founder of the Discalced (unshod) Carmelites, she is barefoot; yet there is nothing naturalistic about the flood of drapery that expresses the turbulence of her soul, while the angel—pure spirit (if perhaps modeled after Bernini's firstborn son)—is dematerialized in folds that crackle like flames. Nor do Teresa's features conjure up that indefatigable founder of sixteen convents who declared that "God walks among the pots and pans." There is nothing mundane about Bernini's depiction of her mystical transport as hard marble achieves an irresistible seduction of the senses.

Bernini's artistic combination of the spiritual and the sensual has elicited mixed responses down the centuries, especially from the neoclassicists and prudish Victorians. Taine and Stendhal raised critical eyebrows at what they considered unabashed eroticism. Even in his own day an anonymous diatribe accused Bernini of "dragging that most pure virgin not only into the third heaven, but into the dirt, to make a Venus not only prostrated but

Bernini, *Ecstasy of St. Teresa*, Santa Maria della Vittoria, Rome
(https://commons.wikimedia.org/wiki/File:Ecstasy_of_Saint_Teresa
_September_2015-2a.jpg)

prostituted." Yet the great majority of the clergy applauded his achievement wherein he "conquered art." Those who were scandalized literally missed the point: Bernini had faithfully translated into three dimensions the saint's own words in her autobiography. They were read aloud at her canonization ceremony in St. Peter's:

> *Beside me, on the left, appeared an angel in bodily form. . . . He was not tall but short, and very beautiful; his face was so aflame that he appeared to be one of the highest rank of angels, who seem to be all on fire. . . . In his hands I saw a great golden spear, and at the iron tip there appeared to be a point of fire. This he plunged into my heart several times so that it penetrated to my entrails. When he pulled it out I felt that he took them with it, and left me utterly consumed by the great love of God. The pain was so severe that it made me utter several moans. The sweetness caused by this intense pain is so extreme that one cannot possibly wish it to cease, nor is one's soul content with anything but God. This is not a physical but a spiritual pain, though the body has some share in it— even a considerable share.*

Since the time the early Church fathers allegorized the Old Testament's erotic "Song of Songs," the vocabulary of sexual love has been understood as the best approximation of the incomparable, ineffable ecstasy of mystics in total communion with God. Just as such an encounter was couched in physical terms, so has Bernini fused in his sculptural ensemble of angel, saint, and billowy cloud (all carved from a single block of stone) several layers of meaning drawn from episodes in Teresa's life. His three key innovations in representing Teresa— her reclining pose, her elevation on a cloud, and the infusion of sensuality—allude, as Irving Lavin has shown, to her death ("in ecstasy," as reported), her frequent levitations (usually following communion at Mass), and her mystical marriage with Christ (whom she addressed, in her last words, as "spouse"). Bernini's literary source was penned by no less an author than the late pope, his patron Urban VIII; his liturgical hymns to Teresa called her transverberation "a sweeter death" and the saint herself a "victim of love" who heard "the voice of her Spouse" beckoning her to "the wedding feast of the Lamb" to receive her "crown of glory." It was left to Bernini, who credited God alone as the author of his inventions, to merge traditional iconography, orthodox theology, and human experience into a unified image of Divine Love.

Bernini returned to the theme of a full-length marble figure of a holy woman in ecstasy a quarter century later in another commission for a small chapel, this time a combined funerary monument and altar work: *Blessed Ludovica Albertoni* (San Francesco a Ripa, Rome). Ludovica was an ancestor of the reigning pope Clement X (Altieri). A widow, she had devoted her life to prayer and serving the poor. At the time of her death in 1553, she was granted an ecstatic vision, which Bernini staged above her altar in the family's burial chapel. Conceived in 1671 following her beatification, the work was completed in 1674.

Ludovica lies on her deathbed and at the threshold of eternity. Carved in the form of a sarcophagus, the marble altar is wedded with the tomb sculpture in a luminous apparition at the end of the small, dark chapel. The walls converge as though wings of a huge triptych have been opened to reveal Bernini's most painterly tableau. With head thrown back, in extremis, lips parted and eyes upturned, she clutches her breast. Physical agony and metaphysical "movements of the soul" resonate through the folds of her dress. White cherubs float like snowflakes down

Bernini, *Blessed Ludovica Albertoni*, San Francesco a Ripa, Rome (https://commons.wikimedia.org/wiki/File:Blessed_Ludovica_Albertoni_by_Gian_Lorenzo_Bernini_(setting).jpg)

streams of daylight from concealed side windows; at the top of the vault, the dove of the Holy Spirit hovers as its symbolic source. Behind Ludovica, Baciccio's painting of paradise with the *Virgin and Child with St. Anne*, to whom the chapel was dedicated, provides a window into Ludovica's vision.

The day before her death from fever, Ludovica received the sacrament and then ordered everyone out of her room. When her servants were finally recalled, "they found her face aflame, but so cheerful

Bernini, *Ludovica Albertoni* (detail), San Francesco a Ripa, Rome (https://commons.wikimedia.org/wiki/File:Cappella_palluzzi-alber toni_di_giacomo_mola_(1622-25),_con_beata_ludovica_alberoni _di_bernini_(1671-75)_e_pala_del_baciccio_(s._anna_e_la _vergine)_05.jpg)

that she seemed to have returned from Paradise." The intimacy—if not the spiritual intent—of the scene to which Bernini admits the viewer was appreciated by the novelist Aldous Huxley, to whom Ludovica's experience seemed so private "that, at first glance, the spectator feels a shock of embarrassment." Allusions to both her physical death and her mystical dying (her ecstatic transport of the previous day) coalesce in a single image, and Ludovica's consummation of death through divine love is shared sacramentally by all who partake of the Eucharist at her altar-tomb.

A comparison with the *St. Teresa* reveals the artist's profound revisions over a quarter century. A tactile apparition has modulated into an ineffable transfiguration—from body into soul. Architectural isolation (Teresa's monumental tabernacle) yields to dramatic immanence as Ludovica's jasper pall cascades toward the spectator like the overflowing stage of Bernini's play *The Flooding of the Tiber*; his special effects anticipate De Mille's or Spielberg's. Diagonals are resolved in sustained horizontals. No family effigies are now introduced as eternal witnesses. Even the choir of cherubs is reduced to a chamber ensemble. The Blessed Ludovica—the embodiment of "the good death," to which Bernini devoted his final meditations six years later—is contemplated by the viewer alone. "Eternal rest grant unto them, O Lord, and let perpetual light shine upon them." This is Bernini's *Requiem*.

The next year, for the Holy Year of 1675, Bernini completed his most widely visited chapel, the Sacrament Chapel in St. Peter's, Rome. Flanked by two exquisite, larger-than-life bronze angels kneeling in prayer, Bernini here provides for all time a vertically staged drama: Christ's sacrifice, liturgically recalled at the altar during the Mass, is superseded a level higher by the gilded bronze tabernacle, the symbolic site of his burial and resurrection. A masterpiece of miniature architecture, its ribbed dome is a revised reduction of Michelangelo's at St. Peter's.

Crowned by a gilded statuette of the Risen Christ (in lieu of a cupola), its drum is encircled by a rhythmic ring of Corinthian pilasters; at the front, two dark windows flank a sunburst of the Holy Spirit (as in Bernini's *Gloria* in the apse of St. Peter's). The gold and lapis columns of the portico are surmounted by bronze statuettes of the twelve apostles, the "pillars of the Church," while Faith and Religion take their place over the main portal. The richly symbolic form of the tabernacle, epitomizing Bernini's architectural ideal for churches,

Bernini, *Sacrament Altar*, St. Peter's, Rome (Charles Scribner)

refers both to the early Christian *Anastasis* formerly erected over Christ's tomb at the church of the Holy Sepulcher in Jerusalem and to Bramante's *tempietto* outside San Pietro in Montorio, on the nearby Gianicolo, the site of St. Peter's martyrdom. As in his first great altar work for St. Peter's, the towering bronze *Baldacchino* over the main altar, Bernini fused references to Christ and his first vicar in a sculptural hybrid: Jerusalem has been spiritually transferred to Rome.

"If you want to see what a man can do, you must give him a problem," Bernini once said. Here again he confronted an "obstacle" (Pietro da Cortona's background altarpiece) and then exploited it by converting it into an integral part of his composition. In this final *bel composto* of painting and sculpture, Pietro's colorful angels now frame the heavenly dome of Bernini's tabernacle (which symbolically eclipses Pietro's globe), while Bernini's sculptured angels are coordinated in scale and placement with the Trinity in the painted heaven, their implicit source. Twice life size, these exquisite apparitions—modeled by the maestro himself—direct the worshippers to the sacramental mystery they embrace. One turns in rapture toward the tabernacle; the other angel beckons the viewer to partake of the eternal.

In his first altar work for St. Peter's, Bernini had raised a huge, sculptural baldachin over an altar, itself above a tomb—of the Apostle Peter. Now in his old age he retranslated sculpture into miniature architecture: a bronze tabernacle in the form of a tomb and raised above an altar. Form and function are equated in this late work, which radiates its creator's faith. Bernini credited God as the source of his ideas; nowhere did he offer more evocative evidence of this belief. His final sculpture, carved in marble as he approached his eightieth birthday, was the most dynamic "portrait" bust of Christ in the history of sculpture, in which, his son Domenico wrote, "he summarized and condensed all his art," adding that his father's "bold conception" more than compensated for the "weakness of his wrist."

Bernini undertook this parting work not for his own tomb, a modest marble slab in Santa Maria Maggiore, but as a gift to Rome's preeminent convert, Queen Christina of Sweden. When she refused to accept it, protesting that she could never afford to repay Bernini for its true worth, he bequeathed it to her in his will. On his deathbed he requested Christina's prayers since she shared "a special language with God." It is precisely through Bernini's special language of gesture and expres-

Bernini, *Salvator Mundi*, San Sebastiano, Rome (https://commons
.wikimedia.org/wiki/File:Bust_of_Jesus_Christ_by_Gianlorenzo
_Bernini.jpg)

sion that his "speaking likeness" of the Risen Lord
conveys its meaning.

The bust was originally mounted on a base
of Sicilian jasper supported and raised aloft by
two kneeling angels on a gilded wooden socle.
Bequeathed by Christina to Innocent XI, the last

of the eight popes Bernini had served, the bust later became the official emblem of the Apostolic Hospital in Rome before disappearing in the eighteenth century. Rediscovered in the sacristy of San Sebastiano fuori le Mura in Rome at the turn of the twenty-first century, it now claims pride of place in the ancient basilica, revealing in full glory Bernini's magnificent sunset in marble. It is well worth making the pilgrimage along the Appian Way. The puzzling, ambiguous gesture—the subject of much conjecture and conflicting interpretations by scholars—was described by Domenico (who surely knew what his father intended) as an "act of blessing." With Bernini, the surface always makes dramatic sense; he was the master of clarity, not ambiguity. Thus the maestro of movement, I submit, left as his parting tour de force not an iconic Christ with his hand raised in a static, formal benediction, but rather a dynamic divine figure shown at the moment he is about to complete the horizontal sweep of the cruciform gesture, a moment familiar to anyone who has attended Mass. In the end, as we should expect from Bernini, it is all about *movement*. Viewed afresh, the bust may come into focus as a Eucharistic apotheosis, a huge white Host elevated as the Bread of Angels, Bernini's sacrament in stone. His career had begun in precocious youth with the posthumous portrait bust of a Roman bishop—a public effigy. Seven decades later, it concluded with a private bust of the Savior animated through marble folds following no natural pattern. The striking realism of the former child prodigy was in the end transfigured by the ethereal vision of a genius for whom life and art were as inseparable as fact and faith.

George Bernard Shaw wrote, "You use a glass mirror to see your face; you use works of art to see your soul." But in the Christian tradition, these works of art—or, more precisely, their *medium*— may shift over time. By the end of the seventeenth century—that is to say, after the death of Bernini— the rich tradition of Baroque religious art, wherein the depth of meaning matched the height of illusion, took off into a flight of decorative fantasy: the Rococo of the eighteenth century.

Kenneth Clark aptly titled this chapter of *Civilisation* "The Pursuit of Happiness." The pilgrimage church of Vierzehnheiligen [Fourteen Saints] near Bamberg is a towering wedding cake of delicious confections in gilded stucco and paint. In his Venetian frescoes and canvases, Tiepolo, the last painter in the "grand style," was to render every Virgin

Vierzehnheiligen church, Bad Staffelstein, Bavaria (https://com
mons.wikimedia.org/wiki/File:Vierzehnheiligen-Basilika3-Asio.JPG)

Mary a Queen—of Heaven no less—as portrayed in his most regal vision of her Immaculate Conception, today in the Prado.

He elevated—often literally on ceilings—with fanfares of pastel colors and light these visions of divinity to an airy, ethereal orbit of weightless delights amid café-au-lait clouds, as we see in his miraculous translation by air-express of the Virgin's house from Nazareth to Loreto in Italy.

The visual arts, in cadenzas of elevated grace, sought above all to delight the senses—and succeeded as brilliantly as they did transiently. However, they rarely stir the soul with any profound insights.

Tiepolo, *Immaculate Conception*, Prado, Madrid (https://www
.wikiart.org/en/giovanni-battista-tiepolo/the-immaculate-concep
tion-1768)

Tiepolo, *House of Loreto*, Getty Museum, Los Angeles (https://com
mons.wikimedia.org/wiki/File:Giovanni_Battista_Tiepolo_(Italian)_-_The
_Miracle_of_the_Holy_House_of_Loreto_-_Google_Art_Project.jpg)

Yet at this dawning of the secular and skeptical Age of Reason the Christian tradition still remained vital and vibrant—in the realm of music.

The greatest music of the eighteenth century was religious. Antonio Vivaldi, whose output and virtuosity rivals Bernini in sound, was ordained a priest; his dispensation to retire early from celebrating masses was sacred music's gain. Ludwig Gerber wrote in his 1792 *Lexicon* of composers that Vivaldi "always had his rosary in his hands and laid it down only when it came time to compose." The Lutheran Johann Sebastian Bach composed masterpieces that represent the musical equivalent of the Sistine Ceiling. His study of Palestrina's Masses offered sufficient grounding in that Roman tradition. Bach's monumental biblical oratorios, the *St. Matthew Passion* and the *St. John Passion*, rival the most profound altarpieces of all time. Indeed, the impeccable German soprano Elisabeth Schwarzkopf, who called herself an *Augenmensch* [visual person], once told me that while singing the *St. Matthew Passion* she would "picture in her mind" Grünewald's famous *Crucifixion* from the *Isenheim Altarpiece* in order to "convey in sound its true feeling and colors."

In addition to so many cantatas—sung to perfection by Schwarzkopf in her early recordings—

Bach composed the magisterial *Mass in B Minor*; it has no peer. Compared with that seasonal favorite Handel's *Messiah*, Bach's *Christmas Oratorio* is more ecclesiastical than operatic; it glows with the flickering of church candles, not the blaze of chandeliers—or footlights. There is a magic to Bach that never wanes; it seems more miraculous at each hearing. He is the master of all sacred music.

But Bach was not without worthy successors. The masses of Haydn and Mozart rank high in the heavens of sacred sound. The devout Haydn has never been underestimated in this realm. His *Seven Last Words of Christ*—originally composed as instrumental counterparts to the biblical readings on Good Friday and then later reworked as a choral piece—may indeed offer the last word on this theme. But Wolfgang Amadeus Mozart was not so fortunate. What bad luck, illness, and a tragically untimely death (at the age of thirty-five) did not do, modern authors have wrought with a vengeance. Will future generations be able to picture this genius as any other than the crude caricature in Peter Shaffer's play and film *Amadeus*: a drunken imbecile with God-given talent and a dippy wife? The common wisdom used to be that Mozart's religious music was merely "for hire," something he knocked off to earn a living so that he could write the music—operas, symphonies, chamber pieces— he really loved. What a surprise, then, to read that his widow, Constanze, said that his favorite genre of all was church music.

A close study of Mozart's sacred music confirms Constanze's claim. His *Vesperae solennes de confessore*, with its twilight "Laudate Dominum," a sunset in sound, was as carefully composed as anything Mozart ever wrote, and it reveals that he paid close attention to the texts of the psalms and canticles that made up the chanted sequences of these vespers. They should be heard in their liturgical context—ideally in a Rococo church by candlelight.

Mozart's glorious *Coronation Mass in C Major* offers a telling footnote, a glimpse into the composer's creative process. The soprano's hauntingly beautiful "Agnus Dei" prefigures its later reworking and recapitulation for the Countess's poignant aria in act three of *The Marriage of Figaro*: *"Dove sono i bei momenti?"*—where have all the sweet moments of love gone? So much for the myth that Mozart recycled bits of opera when composing his church music; here it is precisely the opposite. Both arias begin sorrowfully (as befits the "Lamb of God, who takes away the sins of the world") and then are suddenly transformed into an upbeat conclusion. For Mozart, the peace of *dona nobis pacem* is not a passive one—not the absence of pain or conflict, but rather the consummation of joy.

In the nineteenth century, the Romantic century, artists took to the garrets and painted less for church or court (with rare exceptions) but now primarily for private collectors—and for themselves. Their doctrine of "art for art's sake" took root and replaced the old idea of art as the means for conveying religious truths. (How many Rodins or Monets are to be found in churches?) But the tradition continued to flourish in music—through Beethoven's *Missa Solemnis*, Mendelssohn's Protestant oratorios, Schubert's richly melodic Masses, and Berlioz's *Te Deum* and *Requiem*, down to Fauré's ethereal *Requiem* and the triumphant *Te Deum* of the late Romantic (and equally devout) Anton Bruckner at the close of the century.

Even the anticlerical Giuseppe Verdi was not immune. His *Requiem*, performed and recorded in modern times perhaps more than any other composer's, has rightly been proclaimed his greatest opera. Yet its "Dies Irae" captures in sound the *terribilità* of Michelangelo's *Last Judgment* more faithfully and powerfully than anything before or after—in any medium.

Michelangelo, *Last Judgment*, Sistine Chapel, Rome (https://com mons.wikimedia.org/wiki/File:Last_Judgement_(Michelangelo).jpg)

Its history is one of musical resurrection. As originally planned, it would have been but a fragment of the eventual masterpiece. After the death of Verdi's operatic predecessor Gioachino Rossini in 1868, Verdi proposed as a memorial to that great Italian composer a Requiem Mass, to be composed, sequentially, by a group of Italy's leading musical lights. Verdi's own contribution was the *Libera Me*, the impassioned prayer for absolution: *Libera me, Domine, de morte aeterna in die illa tremenda, quando coeli movendi sunt et terra, dum veneris judicare saeculum per ignem* ["Deliver me, O Lord, from eternal death on that awful day, when the heavens and earth shall be shaken, when thou shalt come to judge the world by fire"]. But the project was scuttled by administrative bickering, and Verdi's contribution lay in limbo for several years.

In May 1873, the great Italian novelist Alessandro Manzoni—author of *The Betrothed* [*I promessi sposi*]—died. Verdi considered him not only one of the finest novelists of all ages but also "a comfort to humanity." As a heartfelt memorial to his literary hero and friend, Verdi completed the *Requiem*, adding all the liturgical movements that culminate in his *Libera Me*. Performed at the first anniversary of Manzoni's death, on May 22, 1874, at the church of San Marco in Milan, it was then repeated at a packed La Scala. The opera house venue permitted wild applause and encores that would have been unseemly in church; at the end, Verdi was given a silver crown.

The Austrian poet, playwright, and librettist Hugo von Hofmannsthal once wrote of art, "Depth must be concealed. Where? On the surface" [*Die Tiefe muß man verstecken. Wo? An der Oberfläche*]. That insight has been applied aptly to the deceptively simple and delightfully "superficial," yet profound, masterpieces of Mozart. Yet it may also explain the enduring achievement of Verdi's *Requiem*. It all rings true right up to that hushed final repeated prayer, "Libera me . . . Libera me." With a subtle stroke of genius, Verdi has the orchestra end quietly on a C-major chord, as if to affirm that the prayer has not been in vain. The late music editor and author George Marek summed it up best: "The *Requiem* is one of those rare religious compositions which are loved both by the faithful and the agnostic. It is also one of those pieces of music which appeal both to the musically literate and the musical beginner. Its beauty lies deep and on the surface."

A word about recordings: I am not surprised to find that I own more recordings of Verdi's *Requiem* than any other piece of music. There is so much room for a variety of interpretations, and a cornucopia of records to prove it. All the great conductors tackle this work. Yet after decades of listening I find myself drawn most to that of an Italian maestro. But it is not the obvious one, Arturo Toscanini, who recorded it several times.

Rather, it is Carlo Maria Giulini, who recorded it with Elisabeth Schwarzkopf's definitive rendition of the soprano's *Libera Me*.

In the words of the Anglican cleric and critic Alec Robertson, "Toscanini's unforgettable interpretation was, at any rate in the *Dies Irae* and *Libera Me*, full of the visionary fervor and fire of an Old Testament prophet. Giulini's belongs to the New Testament. There are stern words in the Gospels about the Last Judgment but the keynote of this [Giulini's] less austere interpretation is compassion—the compassion of Christ."

The musicologist Richard Osborne adds, "It is not necessary to be a practicing Catholic in order to conduct Verdi's sacred music supremely well, though in Giulini's case a fiercely held faith has always been a factor to reckon with, the gentle manner disguising the fires stoked up within." Dame Elisabeth Schwarzkopf, who had earlier recorded (to my ears) the consummate *Nozze di Figaro* under Giulini's baton, commented to me just a few months before she died, "I liked him very much. We all know he fought great battles inside himself to make it right, you see, to find the expression; you could feel it—that he was giving his utmost to do the right thing and never felt safe that it was the right sound; he battled for it all the time, and that brings forth great expression from a human being."

A decade later, Verdi composed the most hauntingly plaintive *Ave Maria* in the history of music: Desdemona's bedtime prayer, charged with the foreboding of danger—indeed, doom (just moments before she is smothered by her jealous husband)—in his late opera *Otello*. It conjures up in sound the Blessed Virgin with more power and presence than any spoken prayer or painted altarpiece. Music and words are here perfectly matched to evoke beauty and simple faith, a pair of velvet gloves. There is an irony here that must be faced: so often Verdi is described as fiercely anticlerical and agnostic, and indeed he often presented himself this way. Yet his final work, composed when he was approaching eighty-five, was his *Quattro Pezzi Sacri* ["Four Sacred Pieces"], which included along with two a cappella hymns to the Virgin— *Ave Maria* and *Laudi alla virgine Maria*—his late masterpieces of choral writing, the *Stabat Mater* and *Te Deum*. Compared with the equally operatic version of the *Stabat Mater* by Rossini, Verdi's is distinctive in his underscoring with meaning every phrase of that thirteenth-century medieval poem about the Crucifixion.

The poem itself is uneven, and Rossini had farmed out to an assistant those verses that he considered weaker; the result is an operatic alternation of arias and choruses. Verdi's, by contrast, is one seamless garment of intense narration, bringing into focus the heroism and horrors of the Crucifixion that begin with Jesus's Mother standing full of grief by the Cross on which her Son has been hung [*Stabat mater dolorosa, juxta crucem lacrimosa, dum pendebat filius*] and concludes its long sequence of images and prayers with the intercession "When my body shall die, grant that my spirit may be given the glory of Paradise." The prayer is full of drama but also divine compassion and humanity. The series of four pieces ends with the thunderous and glorious *Te Deum*, which Richard Osborne rightly claims as the "*Requiem*'s true sequel, a setting which ponders the heights, and scales the depths, of human yearning."

How, then, are we to describe, if not explain, Verdi: brilliant agnostic or, ultimately, if paradoxically, Christian composer? The question is as old as St. John's account of the Doubting Thomas and as modern as those complex characters in the novels of Graham Greene—especially the "whiskey priests" of lost faith in his novel *The Power and the Glory* and his play *The Potting Shed*. How often do those very people who believe they have lost all belief end up praying and giving witness—perhaps more persuasively through the power of doubt—to the last word of faith? Often they end up being the ones who offer others the greatest inspiration, especially if they are touched by divine genius. Like Leonardo (another famous doubter), Verdi gave precise instructions for his church burial. In his case, "one priest, a candle, a cross."

What of the next, our immediate past, century? Religious painting and sculpture offer a few exceptions that prove the rule: the sacred oils of Georges Rouault, evoking stained-glass images of devotion, and the minimalist *Stations of the Cross* by Henri Matisse at the Rosaire Chapel he designed in Vence.

Matisse, Rosaire Chapel, Vence (Charles Scribner)

As the twentieth century traveled through Expressionism and Cubism to Abstraction, the sacred tradition seemed left behind. Even in music, despite some sublime choral works by Benjamin Britten, Henryk Górecki, and John Taverner—and above all Francis Poulenc's soul-searing opera *The Dialogues of the Carmelites*—the tradition has waned. Think of the much-touted *Mass* by Leonard Bernstein that opened the Kennedy Center in 1971 and brought its composer to tears. It is really a theater piece, a "deconstructed" Mass, complete with doubt-ridden celebrant. It fit the times to a "T." Where, then, is the Christian tradition to be sought? In the century's new medium: film. Ours is the age of technology and electronic recordings; perhaps these will provide new means and media for transmitting the tradition.

One masterpiece that stands head and shoulders above all other biblical films is Pier Paolo Pasolini's *The Gospel According to Saint Matthew* (1964). It is stark, minimal, haunting—and hypnotic. The controversial Communist and agnostic director cast a Jesus who was utterly convincing—unlike so many Hollywood epic fantasies. In the bleakness and aridness of the black-and-white setting, Pasolini's Jesus conveys a gaunt, frail physicality charged with

Pasolini, *The Gospel According to Saint Matthew* (Charles Scribner)

spiritual magnetism. His Christ is both real and Reality. The moment of his nailing to the cross is pure pain distilled by acceptance and love, unbearable to watch but impossible to ignore. The grand Technicolor blockbusters from Hollywood do not come close to capturing the faith conveyed by the director who was a self-proclaimed doubter. Perhaps Graham Greene could have put it into words. But the simple subtitles of St. Matthew's own text already said it all.

With audio recordings, the past century has succeeded in preserving for posterity the masterpieces of music (just as film and now digital technology have preserved the visual arts of both past and present). These recordings are themselves works of art—performing art. Arguably the most prolific and painstaking in recorded classical vocal art, Schwarz-kopf once described to me her many long sessions at the EMI studios as a matter of "sculpting in sound." In that respect, she proved the vocal successor to Michelangelo and Bernini. She set a standard.

As for the present state of religious art, it is often hard to be optimistic, and yet there are reasons to remain hopeful. One shining example of what can yet be achieved by a major artist (with an enlightened patron) is Louise Nevelson's 1977 *Chapel of the Good Shepherd* at St. Peter's Church in the former Citicorp midtown complex in New York City.

As a sacred space and sculptural environment, it is peerless on this side of the Atlantic—a worthy successor to Matisse's Rosaire Chapel at Vence. Nevelson's serene white relief sculptures in wood combine her characteristic abstraction with evocative Christian iconography, here translated into symbolic archetypes intended to appeal to visitors of all faiths. She herself called it a spiritual "oasis." The commission was Lutheran; the artist, Jewish. Her achievement was nothing less than an intimate

Nevelson Chapel, St. Peter's, New York (Charles Scribner)

monument, a new jewel reflecting the long Christian tradition in art. In the words of John of Salisbury, "We are dwarfs standing on the shoulders of giants." So our artistic—as well as spiritual—mantra must remain: "Onward."

ACKNOWLEDGMENTS

To my longtime friend and editor-publisher par excellence Michelle Rapkin, I once again owe thanks for her unflagging support and critical editing of my manuscript en route to a publisher. Thanks also to William Handley, Marilyn Lavin, Franco Mormando, and Brian Regan, who read the manuscript and offered insight and encouragement in equal measure. At Rowman & Littlefield, I was triply blessed by my editor Dr. Richard Brown and his associates Jaylene Perez and Patricia Stevenson for their high standards in guiding both book and author along the happy way to publication.

A Note on Notes

Because this essay represents a personal overview rather than an academic treatise, I have decided to forgo endnotes. Yet I owe the reader a few signposts. For more on Michelangelo, see Hibbard (1985); for Haydn and Mozart, I am indebted to H. C. Robbins Landon, from his record notes on Haydn's *Creation* (for Vanguard's Everyman Classics, 1967) to his brilliant myth-breaking book, *1791: Mozart's Last Year* (1988). My own study of Caravaggio's *Supper at Emmaus* may be found in chapter 6 of *Art, Creativity, and the Sacred* (1995). My discussion of Rubens and Bernini is largely drawn from my own two books, which contain the relevant source notes. The best analysis of Bernini's *Ecstasy of St. Teresa*, together with a brilliant study of that artist's creation of the Baroque *Gesamtkunstwerk* [total artwork], remains, four decades later, Irving Lavin's masterpiece of art historical scholarship, *Bernini and the Unity of the Visual Arts* (1980).

George Marek's notes for the 1954 RCA recording (under Toscanini) offer an inviting introduction to Verdi's *Requiem*, with further insights by Richard Osborne found in the current CDs of the 1964 Giulini recording by EMI. My repeated citations— always *forte*, never *piano*—of the soprano Dame Elisabeth Schwarzkopf admittedly reveal a personal prejudice; they may indeed be colored by this author's affection, but she was my vocal standard of perfection long before she became my friend and, some might claim, obsession.

Selected Readings

Apostolos-Cappadona, Diane, ed. *Art, Creativity, and the Sacred.* Revised edition. New York: Continuum, 1995.

Clark, Kenneth. *Civilisation.* New York: Harper & Row, 1969.

———. *Rembrandt and the Italian Renaissance.* New York: New York University Press, 1966.

Ebert-Schifferer, Sybille. *Caravaggio.* Los Angeles: J. Paul Getty Museum, 2012.

Held, Julius S. *The Oil Sketches of Peter Paul Rubens.* Princeton, NJ: Princeton University Press, 1980.

Hibbard, Howard. *Michelangelo.* New York: Harper & Row, 1985.

Lavin, Irving. *Bernini and the Unity of Baroque Art.* New York: Oxford University Press, 1980.

Lavin, Marilyn Aronberg. "Bellini's Frick *Saint Francis* and the Source of the Absent Side Wound." *Artibus et Historiae,* no. 85 (2022): 51–87.

———. *Piero Della Francesca.* New York: Abrams, 1992.

Liese, Kirsten. *Elisabeth Schwarzkopf: From Flower Maiden to Marschallin.* Translated with an epilogue by C. Scribner. New York: Amadeus, 2009.

L'Orange, H. P. *Art Forms and Civic Life in the Late Roman Empire*. Princeton, NJ: Princeton University Press, 1965.

Mâle, Émile. *Religious Art: From the Twelfth to the Eighteenth Centuries*. Princeton, NJ: Princeton University Press, 1983.

Martin, John Rupert. *Baroque*. New York: Harper & Row, 1977.

Mormando, Franco. *Bernini: His Life and His Rome*. Chicago: University of Chicago Press, 2013.

Panofsky, Erwin. *The Life and Art of Albrecht Dürer*. Revised edition. Princeton, NJ: Princeton University Press, 2005.

Robbins Landon, H. C. *1791: Mozart's Last Year*. New York: Schirmer, 1988.

Sadie, Stanley. *Mozart*. New York: Grossman, 1970.

Scribner, Charles, III. *Bernini*. New York: Harry N. Abrams, 1991.

———. *Rubens*. New York: Harry N. Abrams, 1989.

Visser 't Hooft, Willem A. *Rembrandt and the Gospel*. New York: Meridian, 1960.

About the Author

Charles Scribner III received his PhD from Princeton in 1977, was an instructor in the Department of Art and Archaeology, and joined the family publishing house, Charles Scribner's Sons, founded in 1846. His books include *The Triumph of the Eucharist: Tapestries Designed by Rubens* (1982), *Rubens* (1989), *Bernini* (1991), *The Shadow of God* (2006), and *Home by Another Route* (2016). He appeared in two TV documentaries following a successful undercover operation with U.S. Special Agents in Miami in 1991 to recover a stolen Rubens: *The Rubens Robbers* (2003) and *Miami Sting* (2007). His webpage is www.charlesscribner.com.